Nominations and Leadership Development

Empowering Spiritual Leaders for the Mission of the Church

Sandy Jackson
General Board of Discipleship

NOMINATIONS AND LEADERSHIP DEVELOPMENT

Copyright © 2012 by Cokesbury

This book is printed on acid-free paper.

ISBN 978-1-426-73630-8

Some paragraph numbers for and language in the Book of Discipline *may have changed in the 2012 revision, which was published after these Guidelines were printed. We regret any inconvenience.*

MANUFACTURED IN THE UNITED STATES OF AMERICA

Contents

Called to a Ministry of Faithfulness and Vitality

Y ou are so important to the life of the Christian church! You have consented to join with other people of faith who, through the millennia, have sustained the church by extending God's love to others. You have been called and have committed your unique passions, gifts, and abilities to a position of leadership. This Guideline will help you understand the basic elements of that ministry within your own church and within The United Methodist Church.

Leadership in Vital Ministry

Each person is called to ministry by virtue of his or her baptism, and that ministry takes place in all aspects of daily life, both in and outside of the church. Your leadership role requires that you will be a faithful participant in the *mission of the church,* which is to partner with God to **make disciples of Jesus Christ for the transformation of the world.** You will not only engage in your area of ministry, but will also work to empower others to be in ministry as well. The vitality of your church, and the Church as a whole, depends upon the faith, abilities, and actions of all who work together for the glory of God.

Clearly then, as a pastoral leader or leader among the laity, your ministry is not just a "job," but a spiritual endeavor. You are a spiritual leader now, and others will look to you for spiritual leadership. What does this mean?

All persons who follow Jesus are called to grow spiritually through the practice of various Christian habits (or "means of grace") such as prayer, Bible study, private and corporate worship, acts of service, Christian conferencing, and so on. Jesus taught his disciples practices of spiritual growth and leadership that you will model as you guide others. As members of the congregation grow through the means of grace, they will assume their own role in ministry and help others in the same way. This is the cycle of disciple making.

The Church's Vision

While there is one mission—to make disciples of Jesus Christ—the portrait of a successful mission will differ from one congregation to the next. One of your roles is to listen deeply for the guidance and call of God in your own context. In your church, neighborhood, or greater community, what are the greatest needs? How is God calling your congregation to be in a ministry of service and witness where they are? What does vital ministry look like in the life of your congregation and its neighbors? What are the characteristics, traits, and actions that identify a person as a faithful disciple in your context?

This portrait, or vision, is formed when you and the other leaders discern together how your gifts from God come together to fulfill the will of God.

Assessing Your Efforts

We are generally good at deciding what to do, but we sometimes skip the more important first question of what we want to accomplish. Knowing your task (the mission of disciple making) and knowing what results you want (the vision of your church) are the first two steps in a vital ministry. The third step is in knowing how you will assess or measure the results of what you do and who you are (and become) because of what you do. Those measures relate directly to mission and vision, and they are more than just numbers.

One of your leadership tasks will be to take a hard look, with your team, at all the things your ministry area does or plans to do. No doubt they are good and worthy activities; the question is, *"Do these activities and experiences lead people into a mature relationship with God and a life of deeper discipleship?"* That is the business of the church, and the church needs to do what only the church can do. You may need to eliminate or alter some of what you do if it does not measure up to the standard of faithful disciple making. It will be up to your ministry team to establish the specific standards against which you compare all that you do and hope to do. (This Guideline includes further help in establishing goals, strategies, and measures for this area of ministry.)

The Mission of The United Methodist Church

Each local church is unique, yet it is a part of a *connection*, a living organism of the body of Christ. Being a connectional Church means in part that all United Methodist churches are interrelated through the structure and organization of districts, conferences, and jurisdictions in the larger "family" of the denomination. *The Book of Discipline of The United Methodist Church* describes, among other things, the ministry of all United Methodist Christians, the essence of servant ministry and leadership, how to organize and accomplish that ministry, and how our connectional structure works (see especially ¶¶126–138).

Our Church extends way beyond your doorstep; it is a global Church with both local and international presence. You are not alone. The resources of the entire denomination are intended to assist you in ministry. With this help and the partnership of God and one another, the mission continues. You are an integral part of God's church and God's plan!

(For help in addition to this Guideline and the *Book of Discipline*, see "Resources" at the end of your Guideline, www.umc.org, and the other websites listed on the inside back cover.)

Welcome to Your Ministry!

Welcome to your ministry! You have been asked to be involved in the important work of helping persons discover their spiritual gifts and develop their leadership skills in order to serve the world in the name of Jesus Christ. This means that you have been elected by the charge conference to serve as a member of the committee on nominations and leadership development (formerly the nominating committee or committee on lay leadership). This committee or team serves **throughout the year** to guide the church council or alternative structure on matters regarding the leadership of the congregation other than employed staff.

You were elected to serve on this committee because the charge conference considered you to be sensitive to the leadership needs of the congregation and to know the capabilities of the persons in the congregation. By accepting this role, you declare your intent to share your gifts with your congregation and to support and lead it in this way.

This committee's work will affect your life in the church, as well as the lives of others. The influence of the persons you recruit for the various tasks in your church, when elected, will go beyond the bounds of your congregation. These leaders will be representatives of the body of Christ in the surrounding community. Some will represent your congregation in the district and conference structures of The United Methodist Church as well.

The Ministry of Leader Development

according to *The Book of Discipline of The United Methodist Church* (¶258.1) the committee on nominations and leadership development is to:

- **identify** the gifts and strengths of persons in the congregation
- **develop** their gifts and skills and nurture them in their mission or ministry roles
- **deploy** persons according to their gifts and passion in areas of service within the church, community, and world (see also ¶126.)
- **evaluate** the effectiveness of their service and provide necessary training and support
- **monitor** the progress of their development and celebrate their accomplishments and service

Identify

Now there are varieties of gifts, but the same Spirit; and there are varieties of services, but the same Lord; and there are varieties of activities, but it is the same God who activates all of them in everyone. To each is given the manifestation of the Spirit for the common good (1 Corinthians 12:4-7).

For Reflection: Where do you see the Holy Spirit gifting in others? What varieties of gifts, services, and activities do you see?

What process is currently used to identify new leaders or fill the required positions in your congregation? If the committee on nominations and leadership development is functioning more like the formerly named "nominating committee," now is the time to consider a better way of doing things!

SPIRITUAL GIFTS

As Christians, the body of Christ, we all share a common identity in Christ, but we certainly are not all the same. We each have unique gifts, strengths, talents, and abilities that enable us to live out our faith in a wide variety of ways. The apostle Paul explains it this way: "For as in one body we have many members, and not all members have the same function, so we, who are many, are one body in Christ, and individually we are members of one another. We have gifts that differ according to the grace given to us" (Romans 12:4-6). He further explains in 1 Corinthians 12 that there are varieties of gifts for and from the body of Christ, which cannot function without all of the parts working together.

MORE THAN A WARM BODY

It is the role of the committee on nominations and leadership development to help people identify their gifts and understand how they can use their unique combination of gifts in service for Christ *in the world.* For too long, our churches have selected people to fill positions of responsibility only or primarily *in the church,* and we have done even this without regard to the specific spiritual gifts, passion, and preparation of the individuals concerned. Rather, we encourage congregations to use an assessment tool or inventory to help people discover their spiritual gifts and then seek to match them with those needed for a particular position or area of service.

Don't confuse the skills required for secular jobs or professions with spiritual gifts. Although the gifts of the Spirit may be used in anyone's secular job, being skilled at accounting may not be the gift God has given that person for work in the Kingdom. Persons who are teachers by profession may not have the spiritual gift of teaching. When you are thinking about who may lead in your congregation, be sure your process helps you identify persons who have the necessary spiritual gifts regardless of their professional credentials.

CONSIDER PASSION

God not only gives each of us different spiritual gifts but also gives us a compelling desire to make a difference. Passion is another aspect to consider when searching for persons gifted for roles in mission and ministry. What if someone has the spiritual gift for teaching? Should she teach third-grade Sunday school? Perhaps, but perhaps not. He may not have a passion for the spiritual growth of children, but does have passion for community outreach. This gift of teaching may be better used to help others understand the importance of the church's role in reaching out to the world beyond the walls and windows of the church. When spiritual gifts are used in an area of passion, the effects and success can be even greater.

GOD'S PURPOSES, OUR QUALITIES

As members of the body of Christ, we are called to use our gifts, strengths, talents, and abilities in ways that fulfill God's purposes. When this linkage occurs, lives are enriched, mission and ministry ensue, and God's purposes are fulfilled. When this fails to happen, the whole body of Christ suffers.

As a member of the committee on nominations and leadership development, you have the privilege and responsibility to link persons who have gifts to share with opportunities to meet specific needs within your congregation and community. This requires diligence and a strong commitment on your part, but it can be a joyous and rewarding experience.

Perhaps a spiritual gifts assessment can become a part of the new member class or orientation. Offering an assessment regularly can be a way to stay current with the membership and their spiritual gifts. It is also empowering for people to discover that they do indeed have Spirit-given gifts. Imagine the people in your church on fire, ready and willing to use their gifts for service to Christ!

Identify leadership qualities as you consider selecting persons to positions of leadership and service. Remember that not all opportunities for service require extraverted leadership abilities. People who may not be comfortable speaking before a group may do very well in one-on-one situations or behind the scenes. Keep these issues in mind when you are deciding how to deploy persons in ministry.

Develop

For this very reason, you must make every effort to support your faith with goodness, and goodness with knowledge, and knowledge with self-control, and self-control with endurance, and endurance with godliness, and godliness with mutual affection, and mutual affection with love. For if these things are yours and are increasing among you, they keep you from being ineffective and unfruitful in the knowledge of our Lord Jesus Christ" (2 Peter 1:5-8).

For Reflection: How will you support leaders in developing their faith? In what ways does spiritual formation nurture fruitfulness in one's life?

The functions of the committee on nominations and leadership development include more than filling empty slots and passing on those names to the charge conference. The primary purpose of this committee is to help find ways to develop persons' leadership abilities.

EFFECTIVE LEADERS

Effective leaders share several traits. They listen actively to ideas, concerns, or suggestions and express God's love by showing compassion for others through word and deed. They are servant leaders who can both share the work and delegate responsibility. Good leaders are aware of their own gifts and abilities. At the same time, they can recognize the gifts of others and are willing to step aside to let them use their gifts and abilities. They attend to their own spiritual growth and discipleship. In leading meetings, they engage in Christian conferencing and develop agendas that include ample time for biblical reflection, prayer, singing, and so forth.

SPIRITUAL LEADERS

Developing spiritual leaders within the congregation is crucial and should begin with the committee members. You have the opportunity and the privilege to be an example of spiritual leadership. The *Discipline* states that "members of the committee shall engage in and be attentive to developing and enhancing their own Christian spiritual life in light of the mission of the Church" (¶258.1). In order to help others develop in their spirituality, the committee members must themselves engage in Christian spiritual practices that cultivate their relationship with God and participate in study for continuous spiritual growth and leadership skill improvement.

THE MEANS OF GRACE

John Wesley called these spiritual practices or disciplines the **means of grace.** These enable Christians to grow in grace and in relationship with God to become and remain the people that God has called us to be. Just as no runner tries to run a marathon without training and no musician tries to play in a symphony without rehearsing, so no Christian should expect to live well as a disciple of Jesus Christ without practicing the means of grace.

These means of grace are the basics of Christian discipleship. The practice of the means of grace enables Christians to obey the command to love God with all one's heart, soul, strength, and mind; to love one's neighbor as oneself; and to love one another as Christ loves. When we make these means of grace habits in our daily lives, we will grow in holiness of heart and life.

John Wesley mentioned what we now call the "classic" means of grace in the General Rules (*Book of Discipline*, ¶104): The public worship of God, public and private prayer, daily searching the Scriptures, regular (at least weekly) celebration of the Lord's Supper, fasting or abstinence, and Christian conferencing (fellowship and theological/spiritual conversation whose purpose is to find and live out the mind of Christ). The means of grace should also be understood to include outward-directed activities of compassion and justice that also provide us a way to "watch over one another in love." Covenant Discipleship groups, based on Wesley's class meetings, are an excellent way for church leaders and members to practice these "works of piety" and "works of mercy" in a supportive and accountable group. Your committee can encourage participation by modeling it. (For more information on Covenant or Accountable Discipleship see Resources.)

SERVANT LEADERS

As you develop leaders within your congregation, emphasize the importance of becoming a servant leader. Servant leaders serve out of a humble spirit, not out of pride or a sense of importance. When approaching someone regarding a leadership position, be sure to express this as a ministry of service and not simply as an elected position. (If it is that, either change the position into a vital ministry role or eliminate it!) Provide servant leader training sessions to support new leaders in their roles as servants of Christ.

SUPPORT AND TRAINING

When approaching persons to ask them to serve, be sure to let them know what support they will receive as they become a leader. First, commit your committee to pray for each new leader throughout the year. Let "recruits" know that they will have an assigned prayer partner from among the committee leadership or the congregation who will check with them regularly to ask how they are doing and if they have specific prayer concerns.

Follow through with a plan to orient each new person in a position of leadership. Develop an orientation plan and stick to it! There is little that is more frustrating than to assume a new position and not receive adequate orientation to the requirements or expectations. The Guidelines series is one useful tool. Other resources, including PowerPoint™ presentations, are available online (see www.gbod.org/laity.)

Be sure to provide information on training opportunities within your local church, but don't stop there. Also include listings of training events available through the district or annual conference. Encourage people to attend lay academies and perhaps become lay servants. Lay Servants (formerly Lay Speakers) Ministries emphases include leading, caring, and communicating. Most of the Lay Servant courses could be taught as short-term studies, small-group studies, or even as Sunday school classes. They are now labeled *Learning & Leading* for that reason. If persons wish to pursue Lay Servant Ministries, guide them through the process (see ¶¶ 266, 267, 268 of the *Book of Discipline*) and provide services of recognition as they receive lay servant status.

Suggestions for Training and Workshops
- Spiritual Gifts Discovery
- Leadership Skills
- Servant Leadership
- Church Committee Work and Responsibilities
- Appreciative Inquiry, Asset Based Community Development
- Consensus Building, Group Dynamics, and Communication
- Orientation to Other Community Ministries
- Accountable Discipleship
- Spiritual Disciplines
- UM History and Polity

ENCOURAGING OR MENTORING

Walking alongside others to help them find and fulfill their call to ministry is Christian coaching. We find examples of this encouraging or mentoring in the Bible as followers were encouraged, held accountable, and guided in their insights and learning. Eli coached Samuel on listening for God's voice (1 Samuel 3). Nathan confronted King David by helping him become aware of his behavior (2 Samuel 12). Elijah encouraged Elisha to use his prophetic gifts (2 Kings 2). Priscilla and Aquila guided Apollos in proclaiming the good news and supported Paul in his ministry (Acts 18). Barnabas encouraged Paul and others by joining their journeys and sharing their ministries, and Paul, in turn, encouraged Timothy (Acts 15–16). Remember that coaching is not advising or lecturing. It is encouraging, empowering, and challenging others in their discipleship.

Be sure to find ways as individuals, and as the committee as a whole, to show support and encouragement during the year. Celebrate ministries events, and individual accomplishments and recognize incoming and outgoing church officers. (See the Resource list and the Guidelines CD for suggested services.)

Deploy

After this the Lord appointed seventy others and sent them on ahead of him in pairs to every town and place where he himself intended to go. He said to them, "The harvest is plentiful, but the laborers are few; therefore ask the Lord of the harvest to send out laborers into his harvest" (Luke 10:1-2).

For Reflection: Where is God calling you to send laborers? Where does Jesus intend us to go?

As you deploy persons in mission and ministry, begin by discerning the opportunities for mission and ministry and the people whom you will seek to invite into these roles or initiatives. List both the mission and ministry opportunities and the gifts of the people, as well as the roles you must fill according to the *Discipline*. Begin a discernment process to match the gifts of the people with the ministry roles needed. (For information on a discernment process see the Guidelines CD.)

The required positions that are elected by the charge conference include leaders of designated ministries of the church council. The *Discipline* (¶249) requires "at least the following leaders for... basic responsibilities":
1. Chairperson of the church council
2. The committee on nominations and leadership development
3. The committee on pastor-parish relations and its chairperson

4. A chairperson and additional members of the committee on finance; the financial secretary and the church treasurer(s) if not paid employees of the local church
5. Trustees
6. The lay member(s) of the annual conference and lay leader(s)
7. A recording secretary

NEW OPPORTUNITIES

There will likely be other areas of ministry in the church or community that need leadership. The committee on nominations and leadership development should work together with the church council on all the leadership needs within the congregation (*Discipline*, ¶252). The committee on nominations and leadership development may also be requested to find persons with the gifts to represent the local church on district committees.

Keep in mind that the actual gifts, strengths, talents, and abilities of the people may determine mission and ministry opportunities and areas of service. Some people may have gifts that are uniquely suited to a specific mission or ministry opportunity. Do not dismiss the idea of developing a new ministry opportunity when you have the people gifted for and passionate about it. That your congregation may not have offered a particular type of ministry in the past does not mean that it is not the time (God's time) to use the gifts of those who have the desire to serve.

Above all, remember that it is most important to focus *not* on church programs, activities, and filling positions, but rather **on seeing God at work in your congregation and the community and finding ways to join God in that work.** This is done by focusing on prayer and discernment rather than by "fixating" on the next new activity or ministry.

INVITATION

The way you approach people to invite them into ministry or to a new opportunity for mission is important. How do you assess the match between the gifts of the person and the opportunity? Or how do you find a mission or ministry opportunity based on the gifts and passion of the people in your congregation?

Everyone has spiritual gifts. Most people want to "do something," but they may not know what is available or how they can use their gifts for mission and ministry. When a person's gifts are identified and he or she is motivated to act, an opportunity **must** be offered. You have the opportunity through the committee on nominations and leadership development to help persons in your congregation discover their gifts and match them with ministry opportunities or position needs.

This matching can happen from either direction: considering persons and their gifts first, or considering first the kinds of gifts needed in a ministry area. When you and your committee members approach people about these gift/ministry matches, decide how you will invite them to consider the mission and ministry opportunity, and how it fits with their passion and desire to serve. How will you ask them to join in Christ's work? How will you let them know that their gifts are needed? Many people are motivated to act when they believe that what they have to offer is important and valued, so your approach is important.

Take the time to put together some questions to ask people whom you would like to invite into ministry. Instead of giving them your understanding of the needs, ask them what needs they see and how they want to use their gifts to address those needs. Avoid doing this casually. Be deliberate about making an appointment to meet with them as a committee or as individuals for a one-on-one dialogue or a small group conversation. You might invite several people to meet to discuss their gifts and how they might be used to further the mission and ministry of the church. Then discuss the position or ministry needs that exist or that might be created and how their gifts could be used in each.

You can build the bridge between people's gifts and passion and the needs of leadership, mission, and ministry. *When adding people to committees and choosing leaders, make every attempt to ensure diversity of the group. Diversity includes racial, cultural, age, economic status, and gender.*

RECOMMENDATION
When you have matched the gifts and passions of the people with the mission and ministry needs of the church and community and when you have obtained the consent of the potential leaders, you are ready to present these persons to the charge conference. New mission and ministry opportunities discovered should go to the church council first to gain their support.

Confidentiality is an absolute requirement! The committee must covenant to keep the information gathered, opinions heard, and records discussed in confidence. This commitment to privacy shows respect for each individual member. Be sure to discuss and form a covenant agreement on the policy of confidentiality at the first committee meeting—before any discussion of persons or positions.

Evaluate

I appeal to you therefore, brothers and sisters, by the mercies of God, to present your bodies as a living sacrifice, holy and acceptable to God, which is your spiritual worship. Do not be conformed to this world, but be transformed by the renewing of your minds, so that you may discern what is the will of God—what is good and acceptable and perfect" (Romans 12:1-2).

For Reflection: How can you evaluate your mission and ministries in the light of this Scripture passage? How will you work to discern God's will?

As in any process, evaluation is the key to continued success. Develop an evaluation plan to assess the status and effectiveness of the committee on nominations and leadership development work and processes. Include an Appreciative Inquiry approach when evaluating or considering changes.
- What is going well? Appreciating and valuing the work that has been done.
- What might be? Envisioning how it could be even better.
- What should be? Dialoguing about what is important—essentials.
- What will be? Innovating ideas about ways to work in the future—changes that you need to make.

Other Evaluative questions include:
- Are those recruited for leadership positions practicing servant leadership principles?
- Are the missions or ministries they are leading effective? (How do we define "effective"?)
- Has the committee followed through with support and training?
- Are the resources used appropriate? If not, what changes are needed?
- What challenges have you experienced?
- How can your committee function be improved? Are there processes that need to be redesigned or improved?
- Are the committee members following their commitment to spiritual disciplines and confidentiality? If not, how can we improve?

Evaluate the plan as well as the person. The church council or specific ministry groups are responsible for developing an intentional and agreed-upon strategy to achieve your church's ministry goals. Evaluation should then center on whether and how well the leader and committee members have followed the agreed-upon strategies. If you have faithfully followed the plan, but you do not get the results you want, *change the plan.* Acknowledge (even reward) sincere efforts to do what was expected, rather than blame persons for poor results of a faulty plan.

ONGOING ASSESSMENT FOR IMPROVEMENT

Try not to make evaluation a once-a-year assessment. Monitor regularly the progress of your work, to lift up those who are doing good work, and to provide help to those who may be struggling. Don't wait until things are going badly to make changes. Be proactive in the work and assessment of progress of both your committee and the various ministries and leadership over which you have responsibility. Consider scheduling time for formal evaluation of your committee's progress at least quarterly.

Monitor

Do you not know that in a race the runners all compete, but only one receives the prize? Run in such a way that you may win it. Athletes exercise self-control in all things; they do it to receive a perishable wreath, but we an imperishable one (1 Corinthians 9:24-25).

For Reflection: In what ways can you train for this race for the "imperishable wreath"? How can you help others train for it?

Monitoring the mission and ministry needs and opportunities of the church and community is critical because they are ever changing. In your gifts assessment of the people, watch for new gifts, abilities, and passions that may lead to new opportunities for service in the world.

Think of some ways that you can invite the congregation to participate in this process. You might develop a survey or questionnaire asking where the members see gifts and abilities in each other or new mission/ministry opportunities. This kind of tool might be used at the end of each quarter in Sunday school classes and at the end of short or long term studies. Ask for a report of the gifts identified during the closing session of DISCIPLE I.

RECOGNITION

Work as a committee to recognize all areas of mission and ministry occurring either as an official local church program or participation in ministries in the district, annual conference, or surrounding communities. By doing this you will help the congregation gain an understanding that ministry is not just what happens within this particular local church. It will provide a view of the connectional Church at work in the world.

JOINING GOD'S MISSION—DAILY DISCIPLESHIP

Take every opportunity to recognize the many ways that people are in mission and ministry in the work or activities they perform every day. Too many times "ministry" means only things like serving on a committee, singing in the choir, or helping to serve a church dinner. These certainly are valid ministries, but persons have the opportunity to live their faith outside the church every day. This too is ministry.

Whether persons work outside the home, are students, or are stay-at-home parents, every task the people of your church are engaged in may be a form of ministry. How they relate to their coworkers, fellow students, neighbors, or families is a witness to God's love for the world. How they show care and respect and honesty in each assignment or task shows faithfulness to doing their best—whatever they are doing.

You may be able to organize a time during worship that provides a witness to ministry in everyday life. Perhaps a bulletin insert, feature, or newsletter column could be written that describes ways that people in your congregation live their faith at school, work, or other social or community contexts. (For more information on *Joining God's Mission* go to www.gbod.org/laity.)

PASSING THE BATON

A part of monitoring the leadership and ministries of the church is to be aware of how long someone has held a certain position or been on the same committee. Some committees have term limits, while others do not. Leadership in the church should be shared. Those who are experienced and have served faithfully should be recognized and commended but also encouraged to "pass the baton" to new leaders. All persons in leadership should be looking for potential leaders—people who exhibit the gifts and qualities that can be nurtured to develop future leaders. Encourage the leadership in your congregation to look for the "shining eyes" of those who are ready to be mentored into a leadership role. This will help the work of the committee on nominations and leadership development when there are future leaders who are identified by others.

Train those in the current leadership to become mentors or at the very least to help identify potential leaders. No one person should hold a position for an unlimited period of time—be alert to these situations and work to change them. Arrange for mentoring of new leaders by those who have been effective leaders themselves. This could lead to a smoother transition process from year to year.

Conducting Your Ministry

a *nd whatever you do, in word or deed, do everything in the name of the Lord Jesus, giving thanks to God the Father through him* (Colossians 3:17).

For Reflection: In what ways will you honor God as you go about the work of this committee?

Your tasks as a committee are listed in the *Discipline* in ¶258.1 as:
- Engage in biblical and theological reflection on the mission of the Church, and the primary task and the ministries of the local church
- Provide a means of identifying the spiritual gifts and abilities of the membership
- Work with the church council on matters regarding the leadership of the congregation (other than employed staff)
- Focus on mission and ministry as the context for service
- Guide the development and training of spiritual leaders
- Recruit, nurture, and support spiritual leaders
- Assist the church council in assessing changing leadership needs
- Recommend to the charge conference the names of people to serve as officers and leaders of designated ministries

The Committee on Nominations and Leadership Development

There should not be more than nine members on the committee on nominations and leadership development in addition to the pastor and the lay leader. All members must be professing members of the local church. One or more members may be a youth, and at least one member should be a young adult. Including youth and young adults may require you to change the times of your meetings or to provide babysitting, but these are important considerations as you strive for a well-rounded view and representation on the committee. Remember that you are encouraged to have a diverse and inclusive group, including race, culture, economic status, gender, and age (¶258.1.e).

The pastor chairs the committee, and a lay person elected by the charge conference serves as vice chair. The membership is divided into three classes, each elected for a three-year term. This ensures a more stable committee because not everyone is new at the same time. A rotation is suggested in ¶159.1.d of the *Discipline*.

ROLES OF THE CHAIRPERSON (PASTOR) AND VICE CHAIRPERSON (LAY)

- Guide the work of the committee throughout the year; plan the meeting agendas; preside at meetings; and foster an environment for spiritual, creative, and valuable work in the congregation through this committee.
- Maintain close communications between chairperson and vice chairperson.
- Establish and maintain a working relationship with the church council or alternative structure.
- Study the passages in the *Discipline* and other resources that relate to this committee and the Ministry of All Christians, Servant Ministry, and Leadership (¶258.1, and ¶¶126–140).
- Allow for the development of community within the committee by providing ample time for Christian conferencing.
- Share the work and ministry (see *Discipline*, ¶131).

A WORD TO PASTORS

As the pastor of this congregation, you have the opportunity to become familiar with the gifts, talents, and abilities that are manifested in the congregation. You should also be aware of service opportunities and needs in the congregation, the community, and the world through your contacts in the community, district, and annual conference. Work with the committee to discern and match these gifts and ministries. Now is the time to encourage the committee to take a fresh look at these members and the gifts they have to offer. It may be time to choose new leadership. This is your chance to guide the committee in looking at a new way to choose and prepare the non-staff leadership of the congregation. It is important that your own attitude be one of willingness and openness to change as well.

A teamwork approach and delegation of tasks will not only relieve you of much of the work but also instill a sense of purpose in the committee rather than the tendency to "let the pastor do it." Remember that all Christians have been gifted and called through their baptism to be Christ's representatives in the world through a ministry of servanthood (¶126 and Baptismal Covenant I).

NEW PASTORS

As a new pastor you should rely on the committee members' knowledge of the congregation. However, this is also an opportunity to ask insightful questions, to offer alternative suggestions, or to propose new and creative ways of performing the tasks of the committee. Your newness may enable you to notice gifts and strengths in members that others may not have seen. This is a time for you to share your observations with the committee.

Getting Started

The work of the committee on nominations and leadership development continues, rather than ends, after the charge conference. Your committee will work to help persons discover their gifts and ways to be in mission and ministry; train new, existing, and potential leadership; support those who have been elected in their roles; and discern new mission or ministry opportunities. These tasks recur throughout the entire year.

A VISION FOR YOUR WORK

Work together with your committee to develop a vision for your work. Use the Appreciative Inquiry process (see Resources) to maintain a positive focus rather than dwelling on what's wrong or needs to be fixed. Schedule a retreat for the committee to form community and do the work of visioning. Some sample questions to guide your visioning:

- Where do you see God at work in the church, your community, the world?
- How can you join God in that work?

What Would It Look Like?

- If all persons were involved in servant leadership in our congregation, what would it look like? What would they be doing?
- If all persons were being formed as disciples, what would be happening?
- If members were using their gifts and skills faithfully and effectively in the community, what might happen?
- If we helped all members of our congregation to identify their gifts, to understand what God is calling them to do, and to equip themselves for ministry, what would be possible?
- If all leaders were ready to forget former ways and do a new thing (Isaiah 43:18-19), what would be allowed to happen?

BIBLICAL AND THEOLOGICAL REFLECTION

This task can be done at each meeting as you begin the work of your committee. Your reflections/meditations should focus on the mission and ministry of the church and the primary task to make disciples (see Part III, "The Ministry of All Christians: The Mission and Ministry of the Church" ¶¶120-124 and ¶201 in the *Book of Discipline*).

Each meeting can and should be a time of Christian conferencing where the members meditate or reflect on Scripture, share prayer concerns, pray, and possibly sing together. Time is taken to pray over the agenda and to seek discernment or guidance before making decisions. Prayer at the end of the meeting is more than a formality. It is a sincere request that God bless the work accomplished, and bless and keep each member until they meet again.

If the committee is truly about God's work, then it is crucial to seek God's will for the mission and ministry of the church. Tithing the meeting time means that you spend at least one-tenth of the meeting time in biblical reflection, prayer, and the practice of other means of grace.

There are several ways you may meditate on Scripture and discern direction and meaning for your work. Choose Scripture passages that relate to the task of the committee or use the daily lectionary readings.

Lectio Divina is a method for meditating on Scripture that can be used in a group setting. Suggestions on ways to meditate and discern God's will and a sample Christian conferencing format are on the Guidelines CD.

Suggestion: You can use the Scripture references listed in each section of this Guideline for study and reflection during your meetings.

Working Together

How well your committee accomplishes its task depends in part on how well the members work together. You are coworkers with one another and with God, seeking to identify, guide, and nurture the leadership of your church. As committee members, you have assumed a commitment and a responsibility to one another. Your task of overseeing the leadership of your church is crucial to strengthening the body of Christ. You can develop a sense of Christian community by sharing together, reflecting on your faith, and understanding the mission of the people of God.

It is important that this committee work as a team to share and to learn together. Meeting agendas should be formed to maximize the time and yet allow sufficient opportunity for the task of biblical reflection and Christian conferencing. People are more willing to attend meetings at which there is both intentional community formation and work accomplished.

SETTING GROUND RULES

Set ground rules for how you will interact with one another. For example:
- The climate in our meetings is one of warmth, informality, comfort, and hospitality. Our discussions are open and honest.
- We understand our roles and responsibilities. We take responsibility and are accountable for completing assignments.
- Everyone participates. One or two do not dominate the discussion.

- We work for consensus, not necessarily unanimous decisions. We avoid win-lose voting where possible.
- We maintain confidentiality. This helps establish an atmosphere of trust.
- We will use effective listening techniques. We will also provide feedback to the speaker to ensure a clear understanding.
- We may disagree, but we are not disagreeable.
- We establish ground rules for communication. Consider using a mutual invitation model for group discussion.
- We use resources available to us to complete our work efficiently and effectively.
- We assess ourselves and our work frequently to keep track of how we are doing, spiritually and functionally.

Tools for Your Ministry

but *we appeal to you, brothers and sisters, to respect those who labor among you, and have charge of you in the Lord and admonish you; esteem them very highly in love because of their work. Be at peace among yourselves* (1 Thessalonians 5:12-13).

For Reflection: Your work on this committee is invaluable! What tools will you use to ensure that you are doing the best you can?

Set Goals and Objectives
The goals you set will be the means by which you will accomplish your work. Your objectives are the things you will do to meet those goals. By establishing goals and objectives you will establish a framework from which you can evaluate your progress. There are some suggested goals with objectives that follow the assigned tasks of your committee located on the Guidelines CD.

Plan Your Ministry
Another tool to use is the **Planning Guide** which can help you plan and schedule the work of your committee. The guide divides your work into the four quarters of the year with questions to guide your planning, activities to prepare for and accomplish your work and reminders to evaluate and measure the work you have done and that of the ministries and mission areas. This tool is located on the Guidelines CD.

Getting to Know You
Before you can match people effectively with leadership and service opportunities, your committee will need up-to-date information about the gifts, interests, and skills of your members. You might begin with your membership roll and list the qualities, abilities, and interests for each member. In a larger church, an information file can serve as a source to identify persons for elected leadership and service positions, for long- and short-term projects, for behind-the-scenes tasks, and for leadership needs of the community, the district, and the conference.

- Name
- Age and birth date
- Occupation and employer
- Training and education
- Hobbies and special skills
- Special interests
- Address and phone number
- Family relationships
- Spiritual gifts and abilities
- Time available for service
- Church/other experience
- Present participation in worship, Sunday school, and other activities

(See the Leadership Selection Gifts/Skills Databank on the Guidelines CD.)

You can select one or a combination of the following ways to gather this information from your congregation:

1. Survey your congregation through your church newsletter, by direct mail, by phone, or before or after a worship service or a church program. You might also place copies of the survey in pew racks or use the survey as a bulletin insert. Be creative!
2. Interview each church member. (This takes the most time but will give you the best information base.)
3. Gather information on current members during a church-wide emphasis on the stewardship of time and abilities.
4. Gather information on all new members as a routine part of their membership classes or at the time they are received into membership.

KEEP INFORMATION USEFUL AND USABLE

Churches have selected many different methods of storing this type of demographic data. Choose the one that works most efficiently for you, noting that the card file, file drawer, and notebook are time-consuming. Your committee needs to have access to this information, especially at times when you are matching persons with available service opportunities, so **be sure that someone has the responsibility of keeping the information updated.**

• **A card file.** This is one of the most common methods of keeping the information.
• **A file drawer.** The drawer contains a manila folder on each household with an information sheet on each member of the household, no matter how young or how old.
• **A notebook.** A three-ring notebook kept in the church office with an information sheet on each person.
• **Computer records.** Many churches now use a computer to store in a database their financial records, as well as information on the interests, gifts, and skills of each member. Programs such as Google Docs allow for private file editing and sharing over the internet. This method has become the one of choice because of the ease of updating and retrieving information.

Develop a List of Positions for Ministry

Begin by preparing a complete list of positions for which your committee will make nominations. You can prepare your own worksheet (see the CD for a sample). Include all of these positions:

_____ The required positions elected by the charge conference (see the *Discipline*, ¶249). Include members as well as chairpersons for the committees on finance, committee on nominations and leadership development, staff/pastor-parish relations, and the board of trustees.

_____ Other ministry leadership needs requested by the church council (*Discipline,* ¶252), such as Sunday school teachers, persons in ministry with those who have disabilities, the coordinator of scouting ministries, the coordinator of older-adult ministries, the coordinator of single-adult ministries, the coordinator of small-group ministries, a representative to a local ecumenical group, Communion stewards, a committee on church childcare, or a buildings-and-grounds chairperson.

_____ Leadership positions requested by your conference or district—for example, a local church representative to a district organization or a representative for a conference-sponsored United Methodist college.

_____ Officers and leaders of designated ministries of the church council.

Develop Ministry Descriptions

The committee should provide written descriptions of the responsibilities for each position, board, council, or committee to which persons may be elected, appointed, or assigned for ministry. These descriptions make the tasks of inviting and matching persons with positions much easier. More importantly, if individuals have clear expectations about the tasks they will be asked to do and the potential impact, it is easier for them to respond with a sense of confidence and increased commitment.

If you already have descriptions for the leadership positions in your church, be sure they are up-to-date with current leadership needs. *Job Descriptions and Leadership Training for Local Church Leaders* provides a brief summary of the task, information about responsibilities, suggestions about ways to get started, the skills and interests helpful for the ministry, and training that might be available. It also lists references from the *Book of Discipline* and people and agencies that might help for most leadership positions in large or small-membership congregations. The committee should also have the entire set of Guidelines as reference material for the responsibilities of all the elected committees (see Resources).

You may want to practice this process on many emerging kinds of ministries in your congregation or community for which there are no descriptions provided. Revise and update as needed. The following are questions to answer when developing other ministry position descriptions:
   • What do you do (what are your functions and responsibilities)?

- To whom do you report about the ministry work?
- What is the primary objective of your ministry team or service?
- How does it facilitate the primary task of the congregation?
- What gifts, abilities, and special skills does this job require?

Another possible way to develop job descriptions is to ask district or conference groups or other United Methodist churches for descriptions of leadership, mission, and ministry positions similar to those in your church. Then, modify the descriptions to fit your local needs.

Check with the church council for other information such as:
- What training can this leader count on receiving? (The committee on nominations and leadership development needs to be particularly sure about this. If the training will not be adequate, begin planning for the types of growth experiences that the new leaders will need.)
- Where and how does this leader get the resources needed to fulfill the task? For instance, what budget is available; how many other people can be counted on to be a part of the work effort?

Keep copies of the job descriptions on file and update them each year. You will need them each time you ask persons to consider giving their time and gifts.

Selecting and Supporting Leaders

i give thanks to my God always for you because of the grace of God that has been given you in Christ Jesus, for in every way you have been enriched in him, in speech and knowledge of every kind—just as the testimony of Christ has been strengthened among you—so that you are not lacking in any spiritual gift as you wait for the revealing of our Lord Jesus Christ. He will also strengthen you to the end, so that you may be blameless on the day of our Lord Jesus Christ. God is faithful; by him you were called into the fellowship of his Son, Jesus Christ our Lord (1 Corinthians 1:4-9).

For Reflection: Based on this Scripture, how will you select new leaders? How will you support them in their ministries?

Now you are ready to begin the crucial task of selecting leaders and matching them with the available opportunities or helping to create new ones that match their gifts and passion. (See the Suggested Meeting Procedure on the Guidelines CD.) You are entrusted with helping persons find their places in the congregation and in the community. As you offer them opportunities to serve, you are helping them fulfill their calling as disciples of Christ.

Questions to Consider
- Do the persons considered (overall) represent a balance of the economic, social, and theological orientation of our congregation?
- Have we remembered persons with disabilities?
- Have we taken seriously our commitment to maintaining our diversity in the midst of our oneness in Jesus Christ?
- Would they be willing to sign a Leadership Covenant? (See Guidelines CD for sample.)

Throughout the process, be especially aware of those situations where the incumbent has served several terms of office. Ask whether a change should be made, either for the sake of the person or the task. (The *Discipline* forbids some committee members from succeeding themselves, so be sure you are aware of which officers can hold successive terms and which cannot.) In some cases where change seems wise, the committee will need to plan carefully how this move can be interpreted diplomatically to persons not being renominated. If a person is ending long-term service in an area of ministry, it is appropriate to celebrate that ministry, especially if the person is not pursuing another area of ministry.

Inviting People to Serve

A face-to-face meeting is much more satisfactory and conveys the importance of the decision to be made. Use the telephone, instant messaging, text messaging, or email only to set up an appointment.

Train those committee members who are willing to contact the potential nominees so that they understand each step in the process. Roleplaying is a helpful way to practice the recruitment process. Give each person the opportunity to roleplay a visit with a prospective leader. Here are some suggestions for the committee members to roleplay.

- A committee member telephones John Jones to set up an appointment to talk with him about a leadership position. Have two persons roleplay the telephone conversation.
- A committee member arrives at the home of Andrea Ward to talk with her about being church council chairperson. Have two persons roleplay the appointment when Andrea is not interested in serving in that position. Then ask two persons to roleplay the same appointment in which Andrea agrees to serve.

INVITATION TIPS

As a committee, decide who will invite prospective leaders. Arrange a time to talk with the person selected. Both the person and the position are important.

Share the ministry opportunity that is available and how the committee feels that person's gifts are particularly suited for this position. Be honest, clear, and realistic about the responsibilities of the position and what is expected. Such statements as "It won't take much time" or "It's easy" or "You won't have to do very much" are misleading and may be dishonest. These statements also minimize the position as well as the person.

Go over the description and make sure the prospective leader knows the answers to the following questions:

- What are my responsibilities?
- To whom will I report?
- Who gives me information and resources?
- What time commitment will be required?
- Of what other committees does this make me a member?
- With whom will I work?
- How long is the term?

Be positive and enthusiastic when presenting a job opportunity.

Outline the training opportunities and the support the church offers.

Describe the election process. The charge or church conference actually elects persons to positions. If the person being recruited accepts the nomination, his or her name will be given to the charge or church conference as the committee's recommendation. Explain that another person might be nominated from the floor and could be elected to the position.

Discuss the Leadership Covenant they will be asked to sign.

Give the person time to think and pray about the decision.

When persons being invited say no, try to clarify what they mean. Are they unwilling or unable to serve at the present time? Are they not interested in this particular position? Would they be interested in other areas of service? Would they be willing to consider prayerfully and get back to you in a reasonable period of time? Thank them for their consideration and any suggestions they may have offered. Allow them to feel comfortable in saying no to this particular invitation.

Let the committee know the decisions of persons who have been invited.

Be sure that each person considered for a position has been asked and has accepted before announcing nominations.

Give a copy of the "Invitation Checklist" to each person who will be contacting a prospective leader. (A copy of this checklist is available on the Guidelines CD.)

REPORTING TO THE CHARGE CONFERENCE
After potential leaders have been invited, present a list of the recommendations for all positions to the charge conference. Forms are provided in the Official Forms and Records System in Local Churches (available from Cokesbury) for the committee's annual report. Highlight the gifts and skills of each person being recommended. This provides recognition for the individual and also shows how seriously the committee undertook its task.

Preparing an Orientation Packet
The orientation packet should include:
- the objective of the church and the statement of its mission
- the policies and procedures of the church and of the particular position
- a description of the ministry responsibilities

- a calendar of church events for the year
- the times and dates of meetings and events—including training events
- resource materials and appropriate Guidelines
- budget information for the church and for that area of ministry
- the process used to report the work of the committee to others

Support and Recognition

Congregational support, appreciation, and recognition undergirds the ministries of those in leadership positions. Ongoing support encourages those who serve. This is a very important task for the committee. Work closely with the church council to make sure scheduled events acknowledge and recognize leaders and persons in service. Here are some ideas:

1. Keep in touch with persons who serve, through informal and planned conversation, support meetings, and times of evaluation.
2. Begin the church year with a consecration service for persons who serve.
3. Hold an annual service or day of recognition and appreciation.
4. Provide orientation and ongoing training programs.
5. Provide the necessary resources.
6. Acknowledge the progress of each person's work and express appreciation.
7. At the end of the term, thank the outgoing leaders and workers personally and publicly for their ministry in your church and community.

Final Comments

Remember that people are the most valuable resource in the life of a church. With them, and with careful leadership and guidance, the church can effectively proclaim Christ's good news to the world.

The ministry of a local church moves forward, falters, or grinds to a halt based in large part on the work done by your committee. Your task is crucial to the ongoing ministry of your congregation and to the Church as a whole. You will be blessed as you work together cooperatively, trust one another, and remain open to discerning God's guidance at every step of your work.

But this one thing I do: forgetting what lies behind and straining forward to what lies ahead, I press on toward the goal for the prize of the heavenly call of God in Christ Jesus (Philippians 3:13c-14).

Resources

** Denotes our top picks

GENERAL CHURCH RESOURCES
The Book of Discipline of The United Methodist Church (Nashville: The United Methodist Publishing House). Available from Cokesbury.

Guidelines for Leading Your Congregation 2013–2016 (Nashville: Abingdon Press). Available from Cokesbury.

**Job Descriptions and Leadership Training for Local Church Leader,* 2013–2016 (Nashville: Discipleship Resources, 2012. ISBN 978-0-88177-598-3. A set of descriptions for local church offices.

LAY LEADERSHIP RESOURCES
**Concepts in Leadership I and II, Discipleship Resources—PDF format download from www.upperroom.org/bookstore.

**Tools for Lay Leader Selection. Print these forms from the Guidelines CD to use during the leader selection process.
- Leader Selection Worksheet
- Leader Selection Worksheet for Classes
- Leader Selection Gifts/Skills Data bank

**Lay Ministry Equipping Resources Catalog (Nashville: Upper Room Books-1-800-972-0433 Item # M184 (free catalog—shipping charges apply).

OTHER RESOURCES
**Appreciative Inquiry Handbook: For Leaders of Change, 2nd Edition*, by David Cooperrider, Diana Whitney, and Jacqueline Stavros (New York: Amacom, 2008. ISBN 978-1-57675-493-1).

**Becoming Barnabas: The Ministry of Encouragement*, by Paul Moots (Herndon: Alban Institute. ISBN 1-56699-293-1).

Discerning God's Will Together, by Danny E. Morris and Charles M. Olsen (Herndon: Alban Institute, 1998. ISBN 1-56699-177-3).

**Eight Life-Enriching Practices of United Methodists*, by Henry H. Knight III (Nashville: Abingdon Press, 2001. ISBN 978-0-687-08734-1).

Leading a Life with God: The Practice of Spiritual Leadership, by Daniel Wolpert (Nashville: Upper Room Books, 2006. ISBN 978-9-8358-1003-6).

**Spiritual Preparation for Christian Leadership*, by E. Glenn Hinson (Nashville: Upper Room Books, 1999. ISBN 978-0-8358-0888-2).

The Leadership Baton: An Intentional Strategy for Developing Leaders in Your Church, by Rowland Forman, Jeff Jones, and Bruce Miller (Grand Rapids: Zondervan, 2007. ISBN 978-0-310-25301-3).

**Transforming Church Boards into Communities of Spiritual Leaders*, by Charles M. Olsen (Bethesda: Alban Institute, 1995. ISBN 978-1-566-99148-3).

WEBSITES
www.Ladiocese.org/ki (Eric Law—Kaleidoscope Institute)

www.appreciativeinquiry.case.edu. (http://appreciativeinquiry.case.edu)

**www.gbod.org/laity (Nominations and Leadership Development Guideline Power Point Presentation)